Discovery KIDS

Spin-the-Wheel

Extreme

Deserts

LIVE. LEARN. DISCOVER.

PaRragon

Bath · New York · Singapore · Hong Kong · Cologne · Delhi · Melbourne

Dingo

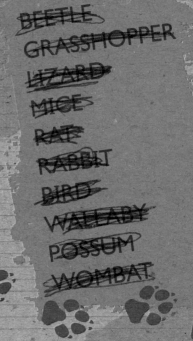

Dingo Word Search

```
L S R A B B I T Y G K
D T B E E T L E B R K
R A D C Y V L T A A H
I R B S T Z C O L S Q
B Y U O N T P C L S J
X H H E J E Q G A H M
J J K L Q R S E W O I
L V Q L I Z A R D P C
G F X T A B M O W P E
V P Q G Y R S B G E C
H P O S S U M W V R F
```

BEETLE
GRASSHOPPER
LIZARD
MICE
RAT
RABBIT
BIRD
WALLABY
POSSUM
WOMBAT

There are ten of the dingo's favorite foods hidden in the squares above. Can you find them all?

Match the Dingo

Which of these shadows matches the dingo below?

The dingo has been native to Australia for up to 5,000 years, but it may have come from Southeast Asia.

Wheel Quiz:

What is the endangered status of the dingo?

a. Low
b. Medium
c. High

Red Kangaroo

Red Kangaroo Math

Do the math to find out some interesting facts about the red kangaroo.

How much does a red kangaroo weigh?
220 − 110 + 88 = ___
Answer: __ pounds.

How long is a newborn joey?
4 + 3 − 6 = ___
Answer: __ inches.

How long is a red kangaroo's tail?
75 + 45 − 81 = ___
Answer: __ inches.

Label the Kangaroo Picture

Fill in the correct words to label the picture.

MOUTH
EARS
EYE
POUCH
CLAWS
FEET

Wheel Quiz:

How long is a red kangaroo?

a. 5.25 feet

b. 6.25 feet

c. 3.7 feet

5

Thorny Devil

Hidden Fact

Cross out the numbers in the table below, then copy the remaining letters into the boxes to discover a special fact about the thorny devil.

3	2	1	4	5	D	5	R	7	5	2	3	3	A	7	2	9	G	8
6	O	3	6	N	9	L	4	I	7	Z	3	A	6	R	4	D	2	S

The thorny devil is a reptile belonging to a family known as the _ _ _ _ _ _ _ _ _ _ _ _ _ .

Thorny Devil

Spot the Difference

Can you find four differences between these two thorny devils?

At night, dew collects on the thorny devil's back and drips into its mouth. It also takes in moisture through its skin.

Wheel Quiz:

What is the thorny devil's favorite food?

a. Spiders
b. Flowers
c. Ants

Spiny Anteater

The spiny anteater has poor vision, but a great sense of smell. Help it find its way to the anthill.

Anteater Maze

Start

Finish

Anteater Snack Attack

If threatened, the spiny anteater rolls itself into a prickly ball with its spines sticking out for protection.

Spiny anteaters mostly eat ants and termites, but will eat other foods, too. Which food is which?

Match the names with the correct food.

Worm

Termite

Ant

Grub

Wheel Quiz:

How big is a spiny anteater?

a. 14–24 inches
b. 13–17 inches
c. 8–10 inches

DiscoveryFact™

In family groups of meerkats, a couple stand on their hind legs, watching out for predators, such as eagles.

Meerkat Odd One Out

Look closely at the meerkats below. One meerkat in each row is different. Put a check next to each one that is different.

Meerkat
True or False

The meerkat is related to the cat family.

True ✓   False ☐

Wheel Quiz:

Where do meerkats live?

a. Africa
b. Australia
c. Asia

This coyote is hungry. Which trail will lead it to the snake to eat?

Coyote Follow the Trail

C

A   B

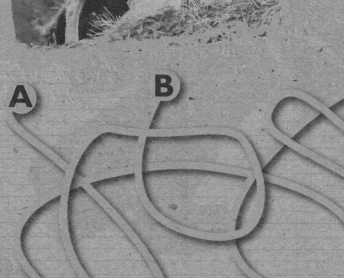

Coyote Calculator Code

Crack the number code to finish the sentence.

The coyote can run up to 40 miles per hour.

1	2	3	4	5	6	7	8	9
A	E	F	I	L	O	P	R	W

The coyote is also known as the
7 8 1 4 8 4 2   9 6 5 3.
_ _ _ _ _ _ _ _   _ _ _ _ .

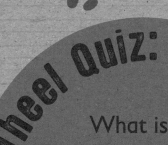

Wheel Quiz:

What is the endangered status of the coyote?

a. Low
b. Medium
c. High

13

Rattlesnake

Can you find five differences between the two pictures above?

Rattlesnake Spot the Difference

DiscoveryFact™

The rattlesnake is the most poisonous snake in North America.

Label the Rattlesnake Picture

Fill in the correct words to label the picture.

_ _ _ _

_ _ _ _

_ _ _ _

_ _ _ _

_ _ _ _

_ _ _ _

MOUTH
EYE
TEETH
SCALES
TAIL
RATTLE

Wheel Quiz:

How long is
a rattlesnake?

a. 24–26 inches
b. 39–54 inches
c. 18–20 inches

Roadrunner Word search

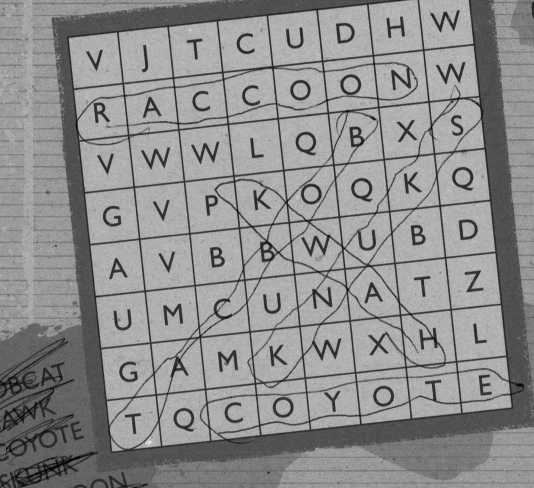

BOBCAT
HAWK
COYOTE
SKUNK
RACCOON

Roadrunners have to run fast to escape from predators. The names of five predators are hidden in the square above. Can you find them all?

16

Roadrunner True or False

The roadrunner is related to the cuckoo.

True ☐ False ☑

The roadrunner prefers running to flying because it can run at 15 miles per hour.

Wheel Quiz:

How tall is the roadrunner?

a. 3.2 feet
b. 2.5 feet
c. 4.3 feet

This jackrabbit is looking for its baby. Which trail will lead it to its baby?

Jackrabbit Trail

A

B

C

Match the Jackrabbit Shadow

The jackrabbit can run at 40–45 miles per hour, and can jump 19 feet.

Which of these shadows matches the jackrabbit?

Wheel Quiz:

Where can you find the black jackrabbit?

a. Mongolia
b. Madagascar
c. Mexico

Leopard Tortoise

Tortoise Spot the Difference

Can you find four differences between the two pictures below?

Tortoise Shell

Draw your own tortoise based on the leopard tortoise. Then make up a name for it.

Desert Animals

Can you find these words hidden in the squares below? They are all types of food eaten by desert animals.

Word Search

Word list:
- ALFALFA
- CACTUS
- EGG
- LIZARD
- LOCUST
- SNAKE
- TERMITE
- THISTLE
- WOMBAT
- GROUNDNUT

I	V	T	E	X	G	G	W	Q	D	A	G
R	Y	E	K	T	L	I	Z	A	R	D	W
X	A	M	A	C	Z	R	A	S	K	O	H
W	T	L	F	V	X	K	X	F	M	S	D
O	H	O	L	A	E	D	R	R	P	X	M
M	I	C	A	O	T	E	R	M	I	T	E
B	S	U	F	V	M	B	E	H	T	M	R
A	T	S	L	J	J	A	J	C	G	G	U
T	L	T	A	E	R	W	V	C	V	G	F
J	E	S	N	A	K	E	O	L	N	E	W
N	G	R	O	U	N	D	N	U	T	S	N
R	S	U	T	C	A	C	I	I	Q	W	M

Desert Food

spiny anteater

Using the words in the word search, can you match the food with the animals that eat it?

alfalfa

pronghorn

coyote

rattlesnake

locust

cactus

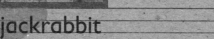

beetle

meerkat

termite

tortoise

jackrabbit

egg

dingo

thistle

ostrich

lizard

snake

23

bustard

Fennec Fox Shadows

Look at the picture below. Then circle the shadow that matches the picture exactly.

The fennec fox has very good hearing—it can hear large insects, such as beetles, walking across sand.

Can you find these words in the squares below? They are all names of foods that the fennec fox eats.

Fox Word Search

W	H	P	F	G	N	A	B	B	T
I	O	M	O	Z	X	L	J	L	I
N	N	R	O	D	E	N	T	I	U
S	R	R	S	S	A	R	G	Q	R
E	V	D	L	N	O	G	G	Y	F
C	Z	Y	Y	A	U	V	A	I	K
T	A	G	G	E	H	L	J	Y	U
B	E	R	R	I	E	S	W	X	O
S	B	I	R	D	K	P	M	V	G
A	R	O	O	T	S	J	C	Y	C

RODENT
INSECT
~~BIRD~~
~~EGG~~
GRASS
~~ROOTS~~
~~FRUIT~~
~~BERRIES~~

Wheel Quiz:

What is the endangered status of the fennec fox?

a. High
b. Low
c. Very high

25

Jerboa Crack the Code

Can you crack the code below?

Use the code breaker to crack the code to find out where in the world you will find the Gobi jerboa.

Matching Jerboas

Two of the jerboas in each row are exactly the same. Check the two that match.

DiscoveryFact™

The jerboa hides in a burrow in the daytime, sealing the entrance with sand to keep the burrow cool.

Wheel Quiz:

Where can you find the Gobi jerboa?

a. Central Asia
b. Central Africa
c. Central Australia

27

Hyena

The Latin name for the hyena is *Hyaena hyaena*. Spell your way across the maze below by coloring the boxes.

Hyena Word Maze

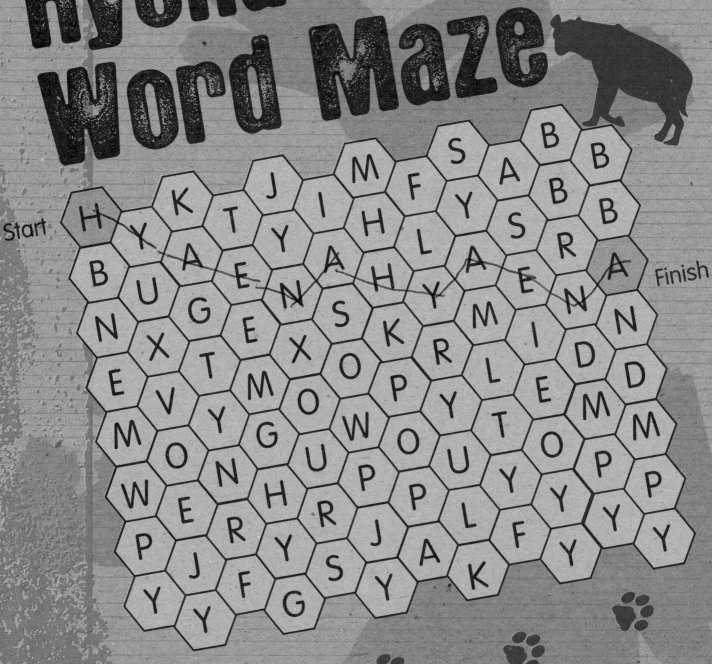

Start

Finish

28

Hyena True or False

The hyena is related to the dog.

True ☐   False ☑

Wheel Quiz:

What is the endangered status of the hyena?

a. High
b. Very High
c. Medium

29

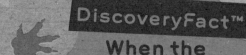

Mongoose

Hidden Fact

Cross out the numbers in the table below, then copy the remaining letters into the boxes to discover a special fact about the yellow mongoose.

4	V	6	E	4	N	4	O	7	M	2	O	3	U	7	S	9	3	8
S	7	N	6	2	9	3	6	A	7	3	3	K	3	E	7	2	S	4

Mongooses will attack and kill _ _ _ _ _ _ _ _ _ _ _ _ _ _ .

Mongoose Mix-Up

Unscramble the letters to finish the sentences.

Mongooses are NDIBL and IRHASLES
_ _ _ _ _ _ and _ _ _ _ _ _ _ _
when born, but their eyes open after a week.

Wheel Quiz:

What is the endangered status of the Yellow mongoose?

a. Low
b. Medium
c. High

Ostrich Close-Up

Take a look at the close-up pictures of parts of an ostrich below. Match the labels with the right picture.

EYE
NECK
WING
LEG
CLAW

Ostrich True or False

The ostrich can't fly, but it can run at 45 miles per hour, the top land speed of any bird.

The ostrich lays the biggest egg in the world.

True ☐   False ☐

Wheel Quiz:

How tall is the ostrich?

a. 5–6 ft.
b. 8.5–12 ft.
c. 7–9.2 ft.

33

Giant Desert Hairy Scorpion

Can you crack the code below?

Scorpion Code Breaker

What do giant desert hairy scorpions use their hairs for? Use the code breaker to crack the code, then write the answer in the space below.

Scorpion Spot the Difference

Can you find four differences between these two giant hairy desert scorpions?

Wheel Quiz:

Where can you find the giant desert hairy scorpion?

a. Malta

b. Mexico

c. Madeira

35

Bactrian Camel

The Bactrian camel stores fat in two humps on its back. It gives energy during long periods without food and water.

Camel Word Maze

The Bactrian camel is an ungulate. Find your way across the maze by coloring in the boxes to spell out 'ungulate'.

Start

Finish

36

Ship of the Desert

Draw your own desert animal transport based on the camel.

Wheel Quiz:

What is the endangered status of the Bactrian camel?

a. High
b. Very High
c. Low

Great Indian Bustard

Bustard Maze

Start

The bustard is trying to protect its egg from predators. Help it find its way back to the nest.

38   Nest

Hidden Bustard Food

Grasshoppers are crunchy and delicious—if you are a great Indian bustard. How many grasshoppers can you find hidden on the page?

The female great Indian bustard lays a single egg once a year in a nest on the ground.

Wheel Quiz:

How tall is the great Indian bustard?

a. 4.8 inches
b. 48 inches
c. 4,880 inches

Desert Iguana

Follow the trail to find out which flower the iguana likes best.

Iguana Trail

A

B

Label the Iguana Picture

MOUTH
~~EYE~~
~~EAR~~
~~TOES~~
~~TAIL~~
~~SCALY SKIN~~
~~CREST~~

CREST

EYE

MOUTH

EAR

TOES

SCALY SKIN

TAIL

DiscoveryFact™

The desert iguana changes color to control its temperature.

Wheel Quiz:

What is the name of the desert iguana's favorite flower?

a. Creosote flower
b. Tar flower
c. Coal flower

Only one of these shadows belongs to the tarantula. Draw a circle around the right one.

Tarantula Shadows

The male tarantula can live for 10 years. The female tarantula can live for 25 years.

Tarantula Word Search

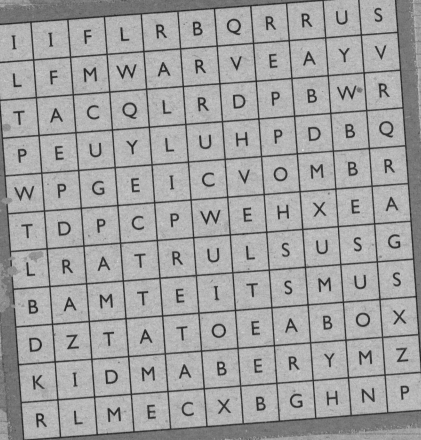

I	I	F	L	R	B	Q	R	R	U	S
L	F	M	W	A	R	V	E	A	Y	V
T	A	C	Q	L	R	D	P	B	W	R
P	E	U	Y	L	U	H	P	D	B	Q
W	P	G	E	I	C	V	O	M	B	R
T	D	P	C	P	W	E	H	X	E	A
L	R	A	T	R	U	L	S	U	S	G
B	A	M	T	E	I	T	S	M	U	S
D	Z	T	A	T	O	E	A	B	O	X
K	I	D	M	A	B	E	R	Y	M	Z
R	L	M	E	C	X	B	G	H	N	P

BEETLE
CATERPILLAR
GRASSHOPPER
LIZARD
MOUSE

Can you find these words in the squares above? They are all names of animals that the tarantula hunts for food.

Wheel Quiz:

What size is a desert tarantula?

a. 2.9–3.7 inches
b. 1.9–2.7 inches
c. 4.9–5.7 inches

QUIZ

How much do you know about desert animals? Try this quiz, then use your wheel to check your answers.

1. Which is tallest?
   a. Ostrich
   b. Roadrunner
   c. Bustard

2. Where does the dingo live?
   a. Australia
   b. Austria
   c. Ireland

3. Which animal is very endangered?
   a. Desert iguana
   b. Gobi jerboa
   c. Spiny anteater

4. Which animal eats only ants?
   a. Thorny devil
   b. Red kangaroo
   c. Leopard tortoise

5. What is the roadrunner's favorite snack?
   a. Lizards
   b. Rats
   c. Vegetables

6. Which animal would you find in Mexico?
   a. Spiny anteater
   b. Black jackrabbit
   c. Fennec fox

7. What is the endangered status of the Bactrian camel?
   a. Medium
   b. High
   c. Very high

8. Which is smallest?
   a. Tarantula
   b. Gobi jerboa
   c. Desert iguana

9. Which animal eats prickly pears?
   a. Hyena
   b. Leopard tortoise
   c. Dingo

10. Which animal would you find in South Africa?
    a. Meerkat
    b. Dingo
    c. Yellow mongoose

ANSWERS

Page 2
Dingo Word Search

Page 3
Match the Shadow

Wheel Quiz
b. Medium

Page 4
Red Kangaroo Math:
198 lbs.; 1 in.; 39 in.

Page 5
Label the Picture

Wheel Quiz a. 5.25 ft long

Page 6
Thorny Devil Hidden Fact:
Dragon lizards

Page 7
Spot the Difference

Wheel Quiz
c. Ants

Page 8
Spiny Anteater Maze

Page 9
Snack Attack

Grub   Ant

Termite   Worm

Wheel Quiz b. 13–17 in.

Page 10
Meerkat Odd One Out

Page 11
True or False: False. They are
related to the mongoose.
Wheel Quiz a. Africa

Page 12
Coyote Follow the Trail:
Trail B

Page 13
Calculator Code: Prairie wolf
Wheel Quiz a. Low

Page 14
Rattlesnake Spot the Difference

Page 15
Label the Picture

Wheel Quiz – 39–54 in. long

Page 16
Roadrunner Word Search

Page 17
True or False:. True. They both
belong to the Cuculidae family.
Wheel Quiz b. 2.5 ft. tall

Page 18
Black Jackrabbit Trail:
Trail B

Page 19
Match the Shadow

Wheel Quiz c. Mexico

Page 20
Tortoise Spot the Difference

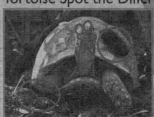

Page 21
Wheel Quiz a: Prickly pear

Page 22
Word Search

Page 23
Termite = Anteater
Lizard = Meerkat
Snake = Coyote
Egg = Rattlesnake
Alfalfa = Jackrabbit
Thistle = Tortoise
Cactus = Pronghorn
Locust = Ostrich
Beetle = Bustard

Page 24
Fennec Fox Shadows

Page 25
Word Search

Wheel Quiz b. Low

Page 26
Jerboa Crack the Code:
It is found in the Gobi
Desert in Mongolia

Page 27
Matching Jerboas

Wheel Quiz a. Central Asia

Page 28
Hyena Word Maze

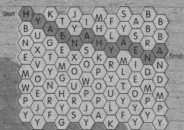

Page 29
True or False: False. The hyena
belongs to the Herpestidae
family, and the dog belongs to the
Canidae family.
Wheel Quiz a. High

Page 30
Mongoose Hidden Fact:
Mongooses will attack and kill
venomous snakes.

Page 31
Yellow Mongoose Mix-Up:
Blind and hairless.
Wheel Quiz a. Low

Page 32
Ostrich
Close-Up

Page 33
True or False: True. An ostrich egg
can be almost 6 in. long, 5 in. wide,
and weigh over 3 lb.
Wheel Quiz c. 7–9.2 ft tall

Page 34
Scorpion Code Breaker:
To detect vibrations in the soil

Page 35
Spot the Difference

Wheel Quiz b. Mexico

Page 36
Camel Word Maze

Page 37
Wheel Quiz b. Very high

Page 38
Bustard Maze

Page 39
Hidden Bustard Food: 12
grasshoppers.
Wheel Quiz b. 48 in. tall

Page 40
Desert Iguana Trail:
Trail C

Page 41
Hidden Bustard Food: 12
Wheel Quiz a. Creosote flower

Page 42
Desert Tarantula Shadows

Page 43
Word Search

Wheel Quiz b. 1.9–2.7 in

Page 44-45
1.a; 2.a; 3.c; 4.a; 5.b; 6.b;
7.c; 8.a; 9.b; 10.c

Credits/ Acknowledgments

Front cover: clockwise from bottom left: istockphoto/ cjmckendry, istockphoto/ Eric Isselée, istockphoto/ John Bell, istockphoto/ kevdog818, istockphoto/ Peter Malsbury, istockphoto/ David Kerkhoff. Back cover: istockphoto / Eric Isselée. Wheel front: istockphoto/ cjmckendry, istockphoto/pamspix, istockphoto/ Denis Peplin, istockphoto/ Jan Gottwald, istockphoto/ Jonas Eriksson, istockphoto/ David Thyberg, istockphoto/ Nico Smit, istockphoto/ Elementalimaging, istockphoto/Andreas Fischer, Dreamstime/Stephen McSweeny. Wheel reverse: istockphoto/kevdog818, istockphoto/ kevdog818, istockphoto/ david kerkhoff, istockphoto/ brytta, istockphoto/ Heiko Grossmann, istockphoto/John Bell, istockphoto/ Peter Malsbury, istockphoto/ John Carnemolla, istockphoto/ Neal McClimon. 2 istockphoto/ Jonas Eriksson, 3 top istockphoto/ Smiley Joanne, 3 bottom istockphoto /Ray Hems, 4 istockphoto Jan Gottwald, 5 istockphoto/ wrangle, 6 istockphoto/ Andreas Fischer, 7 istockphoto/ John Carnemolla, 8 istockphoto/ Shane White, 9 top right istockphoto/ pamspix, 9 bottom right Dreamstime/ Jospeh Calef, Dreamstime/ Will Hayward, istockphoto/ pixelmaniac, istockphoto/ Thomas Perkins, 10 Dreamstime / Veronika Ostrcilova, 11 clockwise from left Dreamstime / cjmckendry, Dreamstime /Veronika Ostrcilova, Dreamstime / Nico Smit, 12 bottom right Dreamstime/ Rusty Dodson, 12 top left istockphoto/Denis Peplin, 13 istockphoto/ Len Tillim, 15 istockphoto/ Maria Dryfhout, 16 istockphoto/ Elementalimaging, 18 top right istockphoto/ Sonya Greer, 18 bottom left istockphoto/ Tim Messick, 19 istockphoto/ Heather Craig, 20 Dreamstime/Patrick Allen, 21 istockphoto/ Nico Smit, 22 Dreamstime/ Jansolo, 23 istockphoto/ Sonya Greer, Dreamstime/ Veronika Ostrcilova, Dreamstime/ Patrick Allen, istockphoto/ Pamspix, istockphoto/ brytta, istockphoto/ Rich Phalin, istockphoto/ Jonas Eriksson, istockphoto/ Len Tillim, istockphoto/ John Carnemolla, 24 Dreamstime/ Nathan4300, 25 istockphoto/ Heiko Grossmann, 29 centre Dreamstime / Erllre, 29 top right istockphoto/ Peter Malsbury, 32 istockphoto/ Lyudmyla Bashtan 33 istockphoto / John Carnemolla, 35 istockphoto / kevdog818, 37 istockphoto/ David Kerkhoff, 38 istockphoto/ brytta, 39 istockphoto/ Tomasz Zachariasz, 40 clockwise from bottom left istockphoto/ Siew Yee Lee, istockphoto/ kevdog818, Dreamstime/ Yulia Ivashkov, Dreamstime/ Yaroslava Polosina, 41 Dreamstime/ Chen Yong Pang, 42 istockphoto/John Bell, 43 istockphoto/ Eric Isselée, 44 istockphoto / Heather Craig, 45 istockphoto / Jonas Eriksson. Font: Hotel Coral Essex by Pennyzine / Jason Ramirez.

Written by Cathy Jones, Consultant Gerald Legg

First published by Parragon in 2010

Parragon
Queen Street House
4 Queen Street
Bath BA1 1HE, UK

ISBN 978-1-4075-9268-8

Printed in Malaysia